POMERANIAN DIARY

2020

Pomeranian Diary 2020

Acknowledgment:

This book is dedicated to animal lovers everywhere.

Henri, the doggy model in this diary, was rehomed as a young adult, happy in his new home, Henri enjoys raising money for a local children's Hospital. In 2018, Henri walked 1000 Miles for charity. You can follow his adventures on Instagram:

Henriwonderdog

Authors proceeds of sales from this Diary will be donated to charity.

https://give.everydayhero.com/au/diaries4kids

Time is set to Coordinated Universal Time Zone (UT±0)

January

Mon 30

Tues 31

Wed 1
New Year's Day

Thurs 2

January

Fri 3

First Quarter Moon in Aries. 4.45 UTC
Quadrantids Meteor Shower. Jan 1st-5th. Peaks night of Jan 3rd.

Sat 4

Sun 5

Notes

January

Mon 6

Tues 7

Wed 8

Thurs 9

January

Fri 10

Full Moon in Cancer. Wolf Moon. 19:21 UTC
Penumbral Lunar Eclipse.

Sat 11

Sun 12

Notes

January

Mon 13

Tues 14

Wed 15

Thurs 16

January

Fri 17

Last Quarter Moon in Libra. 12.58 UTC

Sat 18

Sun 19

Notes

January

Mon 20

Martin Luther King Day

Tues 21

Wed 22

Thurs 23

January

Fri 24

New Moon in Capricorn. 21:42 UTC

Sat 25

Chinese New Year (Rat)

Sun 26

Last Quarter Moon in Scorpio. 21.10 UTC

Notes

January

Mon 27

Tues 28

Weds 29

Thurs 30

Fri 31

Sat 1

Imbolc

Sun 2

First Quarter Moon in Taurus. 1.42 UTC.
Groundhog Day

Notes

February

Mon 3

Tues 4

Weds 5

Thurs 6

February

Fri 7

Sat 8

Sun 9

Full Moon in Leo, Supermoon. Snow Moon. 7:33 UTC

Notes

February

Mon 10

Mercury at largest Eastern Elongation.

Tues 11

Weds 12

Thurs 13

February

Fri 14

Valentine's Day

Sat 15

Last Quarter Moon in Scorpio. 22.17 UTC

Sun 16

Notes

February

Mon 17

Presidents' Day

Tues 18

Mercury Retrograde begins

Weds 19

Thurs 20

February

Fri 21

Sat 22

Sun 23

New Moon in Aquarius. 15:32 UTC

Notes

February

Mon 24

Tues 25

Shrove Tuesday (Mardi Gras)

Weds 26

Ash Wednesday

Thurs 27

February/March

Fri 28

Sat 29

Sun 1

Notes

March

Mon 2

First Quarter Moon in Gemini. 19.57 UTC

Tues 3

Weds 4

Thurs 5

March

Fri 6

Sat 7

Sun 8

Notes

March

Mon 9

Full Moon in Virgo, Supermoon. Worm Moon. 17:48 UTC
Mercury Retrograde ends.
Purim (Begins at sundown)

Tues 10

Purim (Ends at sundown)

Weds 11

Thurs 12

March

Fri 13

Sat 14

Sun 15

Notes

March

| **Mon 16** |
Last Quarter Moon in Sagittarius. 9.34 UTC

| **Tues 17** |
St Patrick's Day

| **Wed 18** |

| **Thurs 19** |

March

Fri 20

Ostara/Spring Equinox. 3:50 UTC

Sat 21

Sun 22

Notes

March

Mon 23

Tues 24

Mercury at most substantial Western Elongation.
Venus at most substantial Eastern Elongation.
New Moon in Aries. 9:28 UTC

Weds 25

Thurs 26

March

Fri 27

Sat 28

Sun 29

Notes

Mon 30

Tues 31

Weds 1

First Quarter Moon in Cancer. 10.21 UTC
All Fools/April Fools Day

Thurs 2

April

Fri 3

Sat 4

Sun 5
Palm Sunday

Notes

April

Mon 6

Tues 7

Weds 8

Full Moon in Libra, Supermoon. Pink Moon. 2:35 UTC
Passover (Begins at sunset)

Thurs 9

April

Fri 10
Good Friday

Sat 11

Sun 12
Easter Sunday

Notes

April

Mon 13

Tues 14

Last Quarter Moon in Capricorn. 22.56 UTC

Weds 15

Thurs 16

Passover ends

April

Fri 17

Orthodox Good Friday

Sat 18

Sun 19

Orthodox Easter

Notes

April

Mon 20

Tues 21

Weds 22

Lyrids Meteor Shower. April 16th-25th. Peaks night of April 22nd.
Earth Day

Thurs 23

New Moon in Taurus. 2:26 UTC
Ramadan Begins

April

Fri 24

Sat 25

Sun 26

Notes

April

Mon 27

Tues 28

Weds 29

Thurs 30
First Quarter Moon in Leo. 20.38 UTC

May

Fri 1

Beltane/May Day

Sat 2

Sun 3

Notes

May

Mon 4

Tues 5

Weds 6

Eta Aquarids Meteor Shower. April 19th - May 28th. Peaks night of May 6th.

Thurs 7

Full Moon in Scorpio, Supermoon. Flower Moon. 10:45 UTC

May

Fri 8

Sat 9

Sun 10
Mother's Day

Notes

May

Last Quarter Moon in Aquarius. 14.03 UTC

May

Fri 15

Sat 16

Sun 17

Notes

May

| **Mon 18** |
Victoria Day (Canada)

| **Tues 19** |

| **Weds 20** |

| **Thurs 21** |

May

Fri 22

New Moon in Taurus. 17:39 UTC

Sat 23

Ramadan Ends

Sun 24

Notes

May

Mon 25

Memorial Day

Tues 26

Weds 27

Thurs 28

Shavuot (Begins at sunset)

May

Fri 29

Sat 30

First Quarter Moon in Virgo. 3.30 UTC
Shavuot (Ends at sunset)

Sun 31

Notes

June

Mon 1

Tues 2

Weds 3

Thurs 4

Mercury at Greatest Eastern Elongation.

June

Fri 5

Full Moon in Sagittarius. Strawberry Moon. 19:12 UTC
Penumbral Lunar Eclipse.

Sat 6

Sun 7

Notes

June

Mon 8

Tues 9

Weds 10

Jupiter at Opposition.

Thurs 11

June

Fri 12

Sat 13

Last Quarter Moon in Pisces. 6.24 UTC

Sun 14

Flag Day

Notes

June

Mon 15

Tues 16

Weds 17

Mercury Retrograde begins.

Thurs 18

June

Fri 19

Sat 20

Sun 21

New Moon in Cancer. 6:41 UTC
Midsummer/Litha Solstice. 21:44 UTC
Annual Solar Eclipse.
Father's Day

Notes

June

Mon 22

Tues 23

Weds 24

Thurs 25

June

Fri 26

Sat 27

Sun 28

First Quarter Moon in Libra. 8.16 UTC

Notes

June/July

Mon 29

Tues 30

Weds 1

Canada Day

Thurs 2

July

Fri 3

Independence Day (observed)

Sat 4

Independence Day

Sun 5

Full Moon in Capricorn. Buck Moon 4:44 UTC
Penumbral Lunar Eclipse.

Notes

July

Mon 6

Tues 7

Weds 8

Thurs 9

July

Fri 10

Sat 11

Sun 12

Last Quarter Moon in Aries. 23.29 UTC
Mercury Retrograde ends.

Notes

July

Mon 13

Tues 14

Jupiter at Opposition.

Weds 15

Thurs 16

July

Fri 17

Sat 18

Sun 19

Notes

July

Mon 20

New Moon in Cancer. 17:33 UTC
Saturn at Opposition.

Tues 21

Weds 22

Mercury at Greatest Western Elongation.

Thurs 23

July

Mon 27

First Quarter Moon in Scorpio. 12.32 UTC

Tues 28

Delta Aquarids Meteor Shower. July 12th – Aug 23rd. Peaks night of July 28th.

Weds 29

Thurs 30

July/August

Fri 31

Sat 1
Lammas/Lughnasadh

Sun 2

Notes

August

Mon 3

Full Moon in Aquarius. Sturgeon Moon. 15:59 UTC

Tue 4

Wed 5

Thurs 6

August

Fri 7

Sat 8

Sun 9

Notes

August

Mon 10

Tues 11

Last Quarter Moon in Taurus. 16.45 UTC.

Weds 12

Perseids Meteor Shower. July 17th to August 24th. Peaks night of Aug 12th.

Thurs 13

Venus at Greatest Western Elongation.

August

Fri 14

Sat 15

Sun 16

Notes

August

Mon 17

Tues 18

Weds 19

New Moon in Leo. 2:41 UTC

Thurs 20

Islamic New Year

August

Fri 21

Sat 22

Sun 23

Notes

August

Mon 24

Tues 25

First Quarter Moon in Scorpio. 17.58 UTC

Weds 26

Thurs 27

August

Fri 28

Sat 29

Sun 30

Notes

August/September

Mon 31

Tues 1

Weds 2

Full Moon in Pisces. Full Corn Moon. 5:22 UTC

Thurs 3

September

Fri 4

Sat 5

Sun 6

Notes

September

Mon 7	

Labor Day

Tues 8	

Weds 9	

Thurs 10	

Last Quarter Moon in Gemini. 9.26 UTC

September

Fri 11

Neptune at Opposition.

Sat 12

Sun 13

Notes

September

Mon 14

Tues 15

Weds 16

Thurs 17

New Moon in Virgo. 11:00 UTC

September

Fri 18

Rosh Hashanah (Begins at sunset)

Sat 19

Sun 20

Rosh Hashanah (Ends at sunset)

Notes

September

Mon 21

International Day of Peace

Tues 22

Mabon/Fall Equinox. 13:31 UTC

Weds 23

Thurs 24

First Quarter Moon in Capricorn. 1.55 UTC

September

Fri 25

Sat 26

Sun 27
Yom Kippur (Begins at sunset)

Notes

September/October

Mon 28

Yom Kippur (Ends at sunset)

Tues 29

Weds 30

Thurs 1

Full Moon in Aries. Harvest Moon. 21:05 UTC
Mercury at Greatest Eastern Elongation.

October

Fri 2

Sukkot (Begins at sunset)

Sat 3

Sun 4

Notes

October

Mon 5

Tues 6

Weds 7

Draconids Meteor Shower. Oct 6th-10th. Peak night of Oct 7th.

Thurs 8

October

Fri 9

Sukkot (Ends at sunset)

Sat 10

Last Quarter Moon in Cancer. 0.39 UTC

Sun 11

Notes

October

Mon 12

Columbus Day
Thanksgiving Day (Canada)
Indigenous People's Day

Tues 13

Mercury Retrograde begins.

Weds 14

Thurs 15

October

Fri 16

New Moon in Libra. 19:31 UTC

Sat 17

Sun 18

Notes

October

Mon 19

Tues 20

Weds 21

Orionids Meteor Shower. Oct 2nd - Nov 7th. Peaks night of Nov 21st.

Thurs 22

October

Fri 23

First Quarter Moon in Capricorn. 13.23 UTC

Sat 24

Sun 25

Notes

October

Tues 27

Weds 28

Thurs 29

October/November

Fri 30

Sat 31

Full Moon, Blue Moon in Taurus. Hunters Moon. 14:49 UTC
Uranus at Opposition.
Samhain/Halloween.

Sun 1

All Saints' Day

Notes

November

Mon 2

Tues 3

Mercury Retrograde ends.

Weds 4

Taurids Meteor Shower. Sept 7th - Dec 10th. Peaks on Nov 4th.

Thurs 5

November

Fri 6

Sat 7

Sun 8

Last Quarter Moon in Leo. 13.46 UTC

Notes

November

Mon 9

Tues 10

Weds 11

Remembrance Day (Canada)
Veterans Day

Thurs 12

November

Fri 13

Sat 14

Sun 15

New Moon in Scorpio. 5:07 UTC

Notes

November

Mon 16

Tues 17

Leonids Meteor Shower. Nov 6th-30th. Peaks night of Nov 17th.

Weds 18

Thurs 19

November

Fri 20

Sat 21

Sun 22

First Quarter Moon in Pisces. 4.45 UTC

Notes

November

Mon 23

Tues 24

Weds 25

Thurs 26
Thanksgiving Day (US)

November

Fri 27

Sat 28

Sun 29

Notes

November/December

Mon 30

Full Moon in Gemini. Beaver Moon. 9:30 UTC
Penumbral Lunar Eclipse.

Tues 1

Weds 2

Thurs 3

December

Fri 4

Sat 5

Sun 6

Notes

December

Mon 7

Tues 8

Last Quarter Moon in Virgo. 0.37 UTC

Weds 9

Thurs 10

Hanukkah (Begins at sunset)

December

Fri 11

Sat 12

Sun 13

Geminids Meteor Shower. Dec 7th-17th. Peaks nights of Dec 13th-15th.

Notes

December

Mon 14

New Moon in Sagittarius. 16:17 UTC

Tues 15

Weds 16

Thurs 17

December

Fri 18

Hanukkah (Ends at sunset)

Sat 19

Sun 20

Notes

December

Mon 21

Ursids Meteor Shower. Dec 17th – 25th. Peaks night of Dec 21st.
Great Conjunction of Jupiter and Saturn.
Yule/ Winter Solstice. 10:02 UTC
First Quarter Moon in Pisces. 23.41 UTC

Tues 22

Weds 23

Thurs 24

December

| **Fri 25** |
Christmas Day

| **Sat 26** |
Boxing Day (Canada & Uk)
Kwanzaa begins

| **Sun 27** |

Notes

December

Mon 28

Tues 29

Weds 30

Full Moon in Cancer. Cold Moon. 3:28 UTC

Thurs 31

New Year's Eve

January

Fri 1

New Year's Day
Kwanzaa ends

Sat 2

Sun 3

Notes

About Henri

Henri was discovered for rehoming on a website called Gumtree in 2017, he was described in the advertisement as unsuitable for young children, but actually, Henri just needed a visit to the vet for desexing and plenty of training. Henri's former family loved him a great deal but were unable to give him the attention needed due to work and family commitments. In his new forever home, Henri has thrived and has been thrilled to be given a chance to give back to the community by raising money and awareness for a local children's hospital. You can follow Henri's adventures on Instagram:

Henriwonderdog

You can follow the fundraising efforts on Everyday Hero
https://give.everydayhero.com/au/diaries4kids

40% of the total sales from this diary will be donated to this fundraising page.

Thank you for your support.